HOLY SMOKE!

We find no jokes in the Gospels, no record of pranks or witticisms shared by Jesus and his followers. The Gospels do show, however, that Jesus shared fully in our human nature — he wept for his friend, Lazarus, and Peter's timid and cautious counsel roused Jesus to indignation and anger: "Get thee behind me, Satan"! (It seems hard on poor old Peter, doesn't it, but it was part of the toughening-up process that would turn him into a rock of faith…)

It is reasonable to assume that Jesus, sharing the tears friends, had the c

Laughter has it life, and it is in t is published.

GW00802217

✠ ✠ ✠ ✠ ✠ ✠ ✠ ✠ ✠ ✠

Reverend Septimus MacGillicuddy O'Reek is the pen-name of a well-known and much-loved Irish priest, who prefers to remain anonymous.

HOLY SMOKE!

The Lighter Side of Faith

Reverend
Septimus MacGillicuddy O'Reek

CAMPUS PUBLISHING

© Copyright Campus Publishing Ltd.

First published November 1993

ISBN 1 873223 11 0

Typesetting by City Print, Galway.
Printed and bound in Ireland by Leinster Leader Printing

Published by
Campus Publishing
26 Tirellan Heights
Galway
Ireland

There was once a very old nun whom the sisters had kept alive for years by giving her a glass of milk laced with brandy a couple of times a day. But at last she came to die. Sadly the nuns gathered around her bed to hear her last words. "Whatever you do, sisters," she advised, "Never get rid of that cow!"

A boat crashed into some rocks and began to sink. "Does anyone know how to pray?" asked the skipper. "Yes, I do," said a zealous Christian, leaping to his feet. "Good," said the skipper, "you pray. The rest of us will put on life-jackets. We're one short!"

✠ ✠ ✠ ✠ ✠

A priest was walking along a street when he saw a little boy jumping up and down, trying to ring a door bell. The poor child was too small and the bell was too high. So the priest went up and rang the bell for the little fellow. Then, turning to the boy with a smile, he asked: "What do we do now?" The little fellow said: "We run like hell, Father!"

Then there was the young girl who was telling her parents all about her First Confession and the penance she received. "I got two Hail Marys," she said, "but I didn't know the second one so I said the first one twice!"

Two nuns went to the supermarket, in a small red Mini car. When they got there, they couldn't find a place to park. One nun said to the other: "You go in and get the groceries and I'll keep driving around until you come out." She did that, but when she came out of the supermarket she couldn't find the nun or the car. She went over to a man nearby and said: "Have you seen a nun in a red Mini?" He replied: "Not since I gave up the drink!"

A man in the front pew fell fast asleep during a very long and boring sermon. An elderly lady who was sitting behind him was so appalled by his behaviour that she hit him on the head with a hymn book. "Hit me again," called out the man, "I can still hear him!"

Once upon a time a priest dreamed he was giving a sermon. Guess what? He finally woke up... and he *was* giving a sermon!

A motor accident occurred in a small town. A crowd surrounded the victim so that the local priest couldn't manage to get close enough to help. Then he hit upon an idea. "I'm a brother of the victim," he cried, "please let me through." The crowd let him pass so that he was able to get right up to the scene of the accident, where he discovered that the victim was a donkey!

Notice seen in church newsletter: "WOMEN'S GROUP SALE OF UNWANTED ITEMS. PLEASE BRING YOUR HUSBANDS."

Did you hear about the woman who took her husband "for better or for worse"? She found that he proved to be far worse than she took him for!

The teacher had been telling the class the story of Jonah and the whale. "Now tell me," she said, "what does that story tell us?" After a pause a little boy in the back row said: "You can't keep a good man down!"

A drunk was rolling around the street when the local priest came up to him. "I'm glad to see you've turned over a new leaf," said the priest. "Me?" said the drunk, amazed. "Yes, I was so thrilled to see you at the prayer meeting last night." "Oh," said the drunk, slowly remembering, "so that's where I was!"

A week later the same drunk was staggering his way home when he came face to face with the same priest. "Drunk again, Murphy!" said the priest. "So am I," said Murphy, "so am I!"

Teacher: "Who lived in the Garden of Eden?"
Pupil: "The Adams Family!"

A man told his parish priest: "My dog died yesterday, Father. Could you please offer a Mass for the repose of his soul?" The priest was outraged. "We don't offer Masses for animals," he said sharply, "try that new denomination down the road. They'll probably pray for your dog." "I really loved that little fellow," the man continued, "and I want to give him a decent send off. But I don't know what is customary to offer on such occasions. Do you think £100 would do?" "Now wait a minute," said the priest, "you never told me your dog was a Catholic!"

✠ ✠ ✠ ✠ ✠

A little boy was listening to a very boring sermon. Suddenly his eye was caught by the red sanctuary lamp. Tugging at his father's sleeve he asked: "Daddy, when the light turns green can we go?"

The refuse collectors called to the parochial house. They noticed a large collection of beer bottles beside the dustbin. "I take it these are all dead," said one of the men. "Aye", said another, "and they didn't die without the priest!"

A Morning Prayer

Give us, Lord, a bit o' sun
A bit o' work and a bit o' fun
Give us in all the struggle and splutter
Our daily bread and a bit o' butter.

Give us health our keep to make,
And a bit to spare for poor folk's sake,
Give us sense, for we are some of us duffers,
And a heart to feel for all that suffers.

Anonymous

A man who had worked on the buses for many years decided to become a priest. Soon after being ordained he was appointed to his first parish. At least one parishioner recognised him as her former bus conductor and she came to wish him well. "You must find it a big change," she said. "Not at all", came the reply, "sure I'm still taking their money and I'm still telling them where to get off!"

A budding convert was being shown around the local Catholic Church. "What's that?", he asked, pointing to the confession box. "Aahh," replied the priest, smiling, "that's the fire escape!"

A carpenter went to confession and told the priest that he had been taking bits of timber from his place of work. "How much?" the priest enquired. "Not too much, Father, just enough to make a garage at the back of the house." "Now", said the priest, "you know that's not right and for your penance I want you to do the Stations of the Cross." "What size do you want them, Father," the carpenter asked, "so that I make sure to get enough wood?"

At the end of a very long and dry sermon a priest announced that he wished to meet the Board of Parishioners in the sacristy after Mass. When it came to the meeting the priest noticed a strange face there. "You're not a member of the Board,"" he said. To which the man in question replied: "I certainly am - I was never more bored in my life!"

Notice outside a cemetery: DUE TO A WORKERS STRIKE THIS CEMETERY WILL BE MAINTAINED BY A SKELETON STAFF.

† † † † †

There was this man who believed in nothing. Heaven, hell, purgatory, limbo — you name it, he didn't believe in it. Finally, death caught up with him and a friend went to the funeral parlour to see him laid out. Later other friends heard all about it: "There he was, a lovely dress suit, snow-white shirt, a white tie, the lot. All dressed up and nowhere to go!"

⳨ ⳨ ⳨ ⳨ ⳨

A visiting preacher was met at the end of Mass with the blunt appraisal of one parishioner: "That's the worst sermon I have ever heard. It was complete rubbish!" The visiting preacher, quite disturbed, told the parish priest that a certain man had said something critical and pointed him out. The P.P. said: "That poor man is not really responsible for what he says. He never has an original thought. He just goes around repeating what everybody else is saying!"

A priest came to work on a temporary basis in a parish that was situated in a very poor part of a big city. The area was so badly neglected that church windows which had been broken by vandals were never replaced. Instead, a piece of cardboard was used to keep out the wind and the rain. Eventually it came to the time when the temporary priest had to leave. During the course of his farewell sermon he compared himself to the piece of cardboard in the window frame. "That cardboard," he said, "is only a temporary measure. It's not a real pane of glass. During my time of standing in here in your parish I have been very much the same." After the Mass a parishioner walked up to the priest and said: "Father, we want you to know that as far as we are concerned you were always a real pane!"

A tailor confessed to the priest that he had stolen some material from his place of work. "That's alright," said the priest, "but you're not to be making a habit of it." "In actual fact," said the tailor, "I was thinking of making a suit!"

✤ ✤ ✤ ✤ ✤

There was a door outside heaven with a notice: ALL HENPECKED HUSBANDS QUEUE HERE. A vast queue stretched to infinity. A few yards along there was another door with the notice: ALL HUSBANDS WHO HAVE LIVED IN PEACE AND CONTENTMENT QUEUE HERE. One rather hunched little figure stood outside. The angel on duty came up to him and asked: "Why are you standing here?" "I don't know really," he laughed nervously, "the wife told me to!"

✢ ✢ ✢ ✢ ✢

A golden rule for all preachers: "If you haven't struck oil after three minutes, stop boring!"

During the course of Mass, and after a very long-winded sermon, a priest was explaining to his parishioners why there was a very obvious plaster on his chin: "I was concentrating so much on my sermon this morning while shaving that I cut myself." After Mass a note was found in the collection plate. It read: "In future, Father, concentrate on the shaving and cut the sermon!"

"Father, I was looking into a mirror," said the girl in confession, "and I decided I was beautiful. Was this a sin?" The priest shook his head. "No my child," he said, "it was a terrible mistake!"

✠ ✠ ✠ ✠ ✠

The priest's car broke down on the way to a wedding ceremony and he was half-an-hour late on arrival. The wedding party was beginning to panic when he arrived, and he was so embarrassed he never forgot the incident. Fifteen years later, he met the husband at a party and said, "I'm so sorry about that horrible fright you got on your wedding day." "So am I," said the man, "I've still got her!"

✝ ✝ ✝ ✝ ✝

The priest had a wooden leg. One day he was in such a terrible hurry that he parked his car on a double yellow line. Hoping to avoid a parking ticket, he wrote a note and left it on his windscreen: "Have pity — wooden leg." The traffic warden left a ticket and a note which said: "No pity — wooden heart!"

The diocese was concluding its preparations for the annual pilgrimage to Knock. All that remained to be decided was who would preach at the Mass in the basilica. The bishop asked for a volunteer from among the priests who were intending to travel. Soon afterwards one man offered his services and the offer was graciously accepted. The man in question was attracted by the prospect of preaching in such exalted circumstances. He was also something of a legend — in his own mind! In the weeks leading up to the pilgrimage he prepared what he considered to be a perfect homily, and he learned it all off by heart. The Gospel of the day was to be the parable of the Prodigal Son and he chose for his point of departure the line, "I will leave this place and go to my father." Eventually the great moment arrived. The preacher approached his Bishop for a blessing and then strode deliberately in the direction of the lectern. Using no notes whatever, he began, in a loud voice: "I will leave this place and go to my father." Then the worst came to pass… His mind went completely blank. Not another word of his prepared script could he recall. So he decided to make a second run at it, this time varying the emphasis so that it might at least sound like a new line: "I will leave this PLACE and go to my father." But to no avail. He then made a third and final attempt, this time putting the emphasis firmly on the word "father". Still nothing. He now knew that he had no choice but to retreat and concede defeat. On his way back to his seat he bowed graciously before the bishop who whispered, "As soon as you get there, make sure and tell the father we were all askin' for him!"

✠ ✠ ✠ ✠ ✠

The local priest was driving down a country road when a second car careered around the bend, spun out of control, and crashed into the priest's car. The driver of the second car staggered over to the priest. "Holy God," said the priest, "you nearly killed me!" "I'm sorry, Father," apologised the man, taking a flask of whiskey from his pocket. "Here, have a drink of this, it'll calm your nerves." "I don't mind if I do," said the priest, taking a generous swig. He took another gulp. "Here," he said, handing the flask back, "have a swig yourself." "Oh, no, Father," said the man calmly, "I'll just wait here till the police arrive!"

The village drunkard staggered up to the parish priest, newspaper in hand, and greeted him politely. The priest, annoyed, ignored the greeting because the man was slightly inebriated. The drunk had come with a purpose, however. "Excuse me, Father," he said, "could you tell me what causes arthritis?" The priest ignored that too. But when the man repeated the question, the priest turned on him impatiently and cried: "Drinking causes arthritis, that's what! Gambling causes arthritis. Chasing loose women causes arthritis…" And only then, too late, he said: "Why do you ask?" To which the drunkard replied: "Because it says right here in the papers that that's what the Pope has!"

A priest was approached one day by an old friend who was down on his luck. The friend asked for the loan of a fiver. "I'd like to help you," said the priest, "but I can't. I have an arrangement with my bank manager which prevents me from giving you a fiver." "What do you mean?" asked the friend. "Well, he promised never to say Mass and I promised never to lend money!"

A Little Boy in Church

He ruffles through his hymn book,
He fumbles with his tie,
He laces up his oxfords,
He overworks a sigh;
He goes through all his pockets,
Engrossed in deep research;
There's no one quite so busy
As a little boy in church.

Thelma Ireland

A little tot, at Mass for the first time, watched the ushers pass the collection plates. When they neared the pew, she piped up so loudly that everyone could hear: "Don't pay for me, Daddy, I'm under five!"

Father Jack McArdle tells the hilarious story of the young boy writing an essay and turning to his father to ask: "Where did I come from?" "Santa Claus brought you," said the father, who didn't believe that all questions really have to be answered. "And where did you come from?" the boy asked. "Oh, the stork brought me," was the father's throw-away answer. "And grand-dad, where did he come from?" The father held his ground firmly and replied: "He was found under a head of cabbage." The young lad returned to his writing and after a while, he closed the copy and went upstairs to bed. The father was puzzled by the sudden end to the questions, so he checked the boy's copy, where he read, "After persistent questioning, it is my firm conclusion that there hasn't been a normal birth in this family for three generations!"

A youthful priest was celebrating the Requiem Mass of one of his parishioners. In his concluding remarks he mentioned that the soul had departed from the body, and he illustrated it with dramatic gestures by pointing to the corpse and declaring: "Folks, what you see here is just the shell — the nut has departed!"

The teacher asked a young boy: "Who knocked down the walls of Jericho?" The child replied immediately: "Well it wasn't me, Miss!" Teacher was not at all amused and after school made a point of meeting the child's mother. "I asked your son in class today a simple question, 'Who knocked down the walls of Jericho?' and he had the cheek to answer, 'Well, it wasn't me, Miss.' What do you have to say about all this?" The mother sprang to her son's defence: "Listen here, if my child said that he didn't knock those walls down, then he didn't knock those walls down!" The teacher, now near exasperation, decided to call to that evening to the child's home and speak with his father. "I asked your son a simple question in school today, 'Who knocked down the walls of Jericho?', and he said 'Well, it wasn't me, Miss'. I then spoke with your wife and told her what he had said and she jumped to his defence immediately. Now, what do you have to say about all this?"

"Listen," said the father, putting his hand into his pocket, "I don't want any trouble. How much did this wall cost anyway?"

✠ ✠ ✠ ✠

A priest went to visit an old man on his death-bed. In giving him the last sacraments, he asked him to summon all the energy he could and renounce the devil and all his works. "Call him all the names you can think of," said the priest. The old man looked worried. "Hold on a minute, Father", he said, "this is no time to be makin' enemies!"

✝ ✝ ✝ ✝ ✝

The Road to Laughtertown

Would ye learn the road to Laughtertown,
O ye who have lost the way?
Would ye have young heart
though your hair be grey?
Go learn from a little child each day,
Go serve his wants and play his play,
And catch the lilt of his laughter gay,
And follow his dancing feet as they stray;
For he knows the road to Laughtertown,
O ye who have lost the way.

Katherine D. Blake

A man who had become critically ill with a heart condition inherited £100,000 from a deceased relative. His wife, thinking the shock of the good news might kill him, asked the parish priest to break the news as gently as possible. "Paddy," the priest began, "isn't £100,000 an awful lot of money?" "It is indeed, Father," Paddy replied. "Now suppose I were to tell you," said the priest, "that you had just inherited a sum of money like that, how do you think you would react?" "Ah sure, Father," said Paddy, "at this stage in my life and with the heart condition and all, I'd have little use for it, so I think I'd give the whole lot to yourself." With that the parish priest took a heart attack himself and died.

The following announcements have been taken directly from church bulletins:

This afternoon there will be a meeting in the north and south ends of the church. Children will be baptised at both ends.

This being Easter Sunday, we will ask the Principal of the Girl's School to come forward and lay an egg on the altar.

It has been said that most church members are 100 percent willing — 50 percent are willing workers and the other 50 percent are willing to let them!

✝ ✝ ✝ ✝ ✝

The teacher had just concluded a review of the day's lesson. "And now, children," she inquired, "who can tell me what we must do before we can expect forgiveness of sin?" There was a pause, but finally one little boy spoke up. "Well," he mused, "first we've got to sin!"

✝ ✝ ✝ ✝ ✝

Epitaph on a hypochondriac's grave: I TOLD YOU I WAS SICK.

✠ ✠ ✠ ✠ ✠

"Now, Statia", the parish priest said to his housekeeper, "remember that when the Archbishop arrives you must say 'Your Grace'." The moment arrived. Statia hurried to the door, opened it, looked at the Archbishop and solemnly said: "Bless us, O Lord, and these thy gifts, which of thy bounty we are about to receive, through Christ our Lord. Amen!"

Another parish priest was trying to impress upon his housekeeper that she must consider the presbytery to be as much her home as his. "Now, Maggie," he said, "I want you always to remember that while we are sharing this house, everything in it belongs as much to you as it does to me." The following week the bishop was in for the annual Confirmation dinner. Halfway through the meal Maggie ran into the room and cried: "Come up, Father, quick! There's a mouse under our bed!"

He who falls in love with himself is not apt to have much competition.

✠ ✠ ✠ ✠ ✠

A mother was having great difficulty getting her son out of bed for Mass on Sunday morning. Finally, in desperation she came to his bedside and pleaded: "Son, there's two very good reasons why you have to get up for Mass. Number one, you're fifty years of age and, number two, you're the priest!"

Then there was the priest who was forever playing golf. And when he wasn't playing golf he was at the races. Each time a parishioner called to the house or rang on the telephone the housekeeper would simply say, "I'm afraid Father is away on a course!"

Shortly after arriving in his new parish Father Murphy was invited for dinner to the home of one of his parishioners. All through the meal young Jimmy kept staring at their guest. He seemed to show particular interest whenever the priest took a drink from his glass of wine. Finally the young lad said: "Mammy, you said that Father Murphy drinks like a fish and he doesn't!"

✠ ✠ ✠ ✠ ✠

A well-known priest addressing a gathering told reporters that as he was making the same speech the following week in a neighbouring town, he did not wish to have anything published. The following day he was horrified to read in the local paper: "Father Smith delivered an excellent lecture — he told some wonderful stories — unfortunately they cannot be published".

A priest gave an unusual sermon one day, using a peanut to make several important points about the wisdom of God in nature. One of his parishioners greeted him at the door and said: "Very interesting, Father. Today we learned an awful lot from a nut!"

What two things are most helped by shortening? Biscuits and sermons.

Nervous breakdowns are hereditary: we get them from our children.

The bishop was visiting a small school in a very rural part of his diocese, and he was trying to explain to the children in simple terms how his role was a pastoral one. "Now children," he said, "suppose there is a flock of sheep out in the field. What would you expect to find in the middle of them?" One young boy at the back put his hand up immediately: "A ram, me Lord!"

I'm an atheist, thank God!

Keep smiling. It makes everyone wonder what you're up to.

Speak well of your enemies. After all, you made them.

Nothing is all wrong. Even a clock that has stopped running is right twice a day.

✝ ✝ ✝ ✝ ✝

The preacher was outlining the service to the organist. "And when I get through with my sermon, I'll ask those of the congregation who want to contribute toward the Building fund to stand up. At this stage, you play the appropriate music." "What do you mean, 'appropriate music'?" asked the organist. "The National anthem of course!" he replied.

The Presbyterian minister had been summoned to the bedside of a Methodist woman who was quite ill. As he approached the house, he met the woman's little daughter and said to her: "I'm very glad your mother thought of me in her illness. Is your minister out of town?" "No," answered the child. "He's at home, but we thought it might be something contagious, and we didn't want to expose him to it."

⊞ ⊞ ⊞ ⊞

A burglar entered the curate's house at midnight. Drawing his weapon, he said: "If you stir, you're a dead man. I'm hunting for your money." "Let me get up and turn on the light," said the curate, "and I'll hunt with you!"

✟ ✟ ✟ ✟ ✟

The priest came out to begin the Sunday Mass and discovered that his microphone didn't seem to be functioning properly. "There's something wrong with this microphone," he began. To which the people responded, "And also with you!"

A certain parish found itself burdened with a very tedious, pious, and self-centred priest for a couple of years. Then came the day when he was called to another assignment. He announced his transfer by saying: "My dear people, the same Lord who sent me to you is now calling me away." There was a moment's silence and suddenly the congregation rose as one and began to sing *What a Friend We Have in Jesus.*

A preacher who always read his sermons placed his manuscript on the pulpit about half an hour before the Mass was due to begin. One of the altar servers decided to play a practical joke and removed the last page. Preaching vigorously, the priest came to the words, "So Adam said to Eve…" Turning the page, he was horrified to discover the final page was missing. As he shuffled through the other pages, he gained a little time by repeating, "So Adam said to Eve…" Then in a low voice, which the microphone carried to every part of the church, he added: "There seems to be a leaf missing."

The missioner thundered from the pulpit: "Every man, woman, and child in this parish must one day die." With these words he struck fear into the hearts of all his listeners, except for one. Right in the front row there sat a small man, who seemed highly amused by what the missioner had said. His amusement didn't escape the notice of the preacher, who decided to repeat his message and this time with some extra feeling: "Every man, woman, and child in this parish must one day die," he roared. At this point the man in the front seat couldn't contain himself any longer and he burst out laughing. This brought the missioner down from the pulpit for a face-to-face confrontation. "Did you not hear what I said just now?" he boomed. "Every man, woman, and child in this parish must one day die!" " Of course I heard what you said, Father," replied the man, "but you see I'm not from this parish!"

An old lady whose sight was failing sat for hours watching her fish tank. Eventually, she turned to her husband. "Same old rubbish," she complained, "nothing but sex and violence."

There was a time when all monasteries observed a strict rule of silence. In one monastery a monk was allowed to say only two words every five years, and those would be to the abbot. After his first five years of silence, one monk said, "Food cold." At the end of five more years he said, "Bed hard." Finally, after his fifteenth year in the monastery, he said: "I quit." "And I'm not surprised," said the abbot, "all you've done is complain since you got here!"

There was an old woman who crossed the border between Northern Ireland and the Republic of Ireland each day at the same time. She travelled on a scooter with a sack of sand behind her. The soldier emptied the sack and , indeed, it contained nothing but sand. And so it went on for a month. One day, the soldier said to the old woman: "I promise not to say anything to the police, but just tell me: are you smuggling or not?" "Yes," she answered truthfully. "Well, what are you smuggling?" he pressed her. With a smile, she replied: "Scooters!"

✠ ✠ ✠ ✠ ✠

Several priests from a small town were out fishing in a boat. As the fish weren't biting, they fell to talking. Since they had told their parishioners for years that confession is good for the soul, they decided they would practice what they had been preaching. Each agreed to confess his secret sin to the others.

The first said that his great fault was language; he still had trouble once in a while holding back improper words. The second priest admitted that his weakness was materialism: he was too fond of money and it was his first and main consideration in changing parishes. The third broke the news of an addiction to petty gambling on anything from golf to football to horse racing.

The last priest, who was the helmsman on the small craft, had by this time, turned the boat toward shore and had increased the speed. One of the confessors said: "What's the hurry? Besides you haven't made your confession yet." The priest replied: "Well you see, my sin is gossip and I just can't wait to get home!"

The only way to succeed in life is to follow the advice you give to others.

Prayer For Laughter

Lord, how glorious and infectious laughter
can be!
Not the hollow laughter of the fool,
or the humourless laughter of the snob,
but the genuine, spontaneous laughter
invoked by the things we see and hear and
talk about.
Thank you, Lord, for the gift of laughter.
And as life goes on,
give us plenty of fresh things to laugh at,
and save us from taking ourselves too seriously.

Canon Frank Colquhoun

A priest was accosted by a mugger while walking down a dark alley. The thief demanded his wallet. As the priest opened his coat to reach for his wallet, the would-be mugger saw the collar and realised he was robbing a priest. He immediately apologised and said: "Forget it, Father. Keep your money. I had no idea you were a priest." Both nervous and relieved, the priest took out a cigarette and offered one to the stranger. "No, thank you," the robber said, "I gave up smoking for Lent."

A tourist came too close to the edge of a cliff, lost his footing and plunged over the side, clawing and scratching to save himself. Somehow he was able to grab hold of a small bush. Filled with terror, he called out: "Is there anyone up there? Can anyone help me?" He heard a reassuring voice say: "I'm here, the Lord your God." The man said: "I am so glad you came along, I can't hold on much longer." The Lord said: "But do you believe in me?" The man was getting more desperate: "Lord, you can't believe how much I believe in you." The Lord said: "Good. Now let go of the branch." The man stammered, "But, Lord... " And the voice of the Lord came back: "If you really believe in me, let go of the branch." The man was silent for a minute and then yelled: "Is there anyone else up there?"

✠ ✠ ✠ ✠ ✠

A great mystic in the last century visited Jerusalem where he met the Chief Rabbi of his country. "Tell me," said the Chief Rabbi, "what's this I hear someone saying, that you might be the Messiah? What makes you believe such a thing?" "Ah," replied the mystic, with a modest bow, "I had a message from God telling me!" "Funny," said the Chief Rabbi, " I don't remember sending such a message."

Prayer For a Sense of Humour

Give us a sense of humour, Lord,
and also things to laugh about. Give us the grace to
take a joke against ourselves,
and to see the funny side of the things we do.
Save us from annoyance, bad temper,
resentfulness against our friends.
Help us to laugh even in the face of trouble.
Fill our minds with the love of Jesus:
for his name's sake. Amen.

A.G. Bullivant

A little boy was kneeling beside his bed with his mother and grandmother and softly saying his prayers: "Dear God, please bless Mammy and Daddy and all the family and please give me a good night's sleep." Suddenly he looked up and shouted: "AND DON'T FORGET TO GIVE ME A COMPUTER FOR MY BIRTHDAY!" "There's no need to shout like that," said his mother, "God isn't deaf." "No," said the little boy, "but Granny is!"

Once upon a time there were two hurling fanatics sitting at a bar counter, reliving the latest game they had seen. After a brief lull in the conversation, one said to the other: "I wonder is there hurling in heaven?" His friend said that nobody knew for sure, but suggested that they should make a pact there and then that whichever of them died first would come back and tell the other. They both agreed and the pact was soon sealed with another round of drinks.

In due course one of the men died and the day after being buried he turned up at the foot of his friend's bed as arranged. The man in the bed almost died himself with fright, but soon remembered the purpose of the visit. He sat up immediately, eager to hear the news. "Tell me quick," he said, "is there hurling in heaven?" The dead man replied: "Well, I have good news and I have bad news. The good news is that, yes, there's hurling in heaven alright. But the bad news is that there's a game next Wednesday and you're playing full-back!"

Beware of half-truths. You may have hold of the wrong half!

Father Colm Kilcoyne tells a story that is set in the female surgical ward of a general hospital in the west of Ireland. It was a ward noted for the easy-going way which patients and staff had with each other. However, each new admission presented the possibility of either maintaining or disturbing the peace. Things were going fine for a long time until, one day, and elderly lady arrived on the scene. Everyone watched with fascination and waited with anticipation as she sat up in the bed and produced a large plastic bag. Then she started to empty the contents on to the bedside locker.

First she withdrew all kinds of religious objects — statues, scapulars, crosses, prayer books, and enough holy water for a baptism by immersion! Next she pulled out all sorts of tablets and medicines, of every shape, size, and colour.

In the days that followed she would go from the religious objects to the medicinal compounds and back again, while everyone looked on. But there was something else about this lady that was to have a far greater impact on her surroundings. She simply could not be pleased. One day the vegetables were over-cooked, the next day they were under-cooked. One minute the bed was too hard, the next minute the bed was too soft. And so it continued, until in the end she had managed to make enemies of everyone.

Things finally came to a head in the still of the night. She cried out for the nurse and complained bitterly yet again. "There's an oul' wan down there," she said, "and she's snoring her head off and I can't get a wink of sleep. What harm but the doctor told me that unless I got a solid eight hours sleep every night I had no hope of regaining my health and my strength." Coming up for air she continued: "At the same time I know that I'm not long for this world, and in a very short space of time I expect to be spending eternity with my God."

With that, another voice rang out from a bed at the opposite end of the ward, expressing the sentiments of all: "Poor God!"

A mother was entertaining guests when her five-year old son began talking to a fly. "Do you know that God loves you, little fly?" he asked, gently. Everyone was deeply touched by this. "And do you love God, little fly?" said the budding St. Francis. The boy's mother had tears in her eyes. "Would you like to go to God, little fly?" the boy persisted. The guests looked at him in admiration. "Then go to God, little fly!" said the boy and squashed it.

A man was bothered with continual ringing in his ears, bulging eyes, and a flushed face. Over a period of three years he went to one doctor after another. One took out his tonsils, one removed his appendix, another pulled all his teeth. Finally, one doctor told him that there was no hope — he had six months to live.

The poor fellow quit his job, sold all his belongings and decided to live it up before he went to meet his maker. He went to his tailor and ordered several suits and shirts. The tailor measured his neck and wrote down "$16\frac{1}{2}$". The man corrected him. "It's $15\frac{1}{2}$," he said. The tailor measured again — $16\frac{1}{2}$. But the man insisted that he had always worn a size $15\frac{1}{2}$. "Well, alright," said the tailor, "just don't come back here complaining if you have ringing ears, bulging eyes and a flushed face!"

Two women are standing beside the corpse at a wake. One says to the other: "Doesn't he look so peaceful and serene?" The other replies: "That's because he doesn't know he's dead yet." "Well," concludes the first, "when he wakes up the shock will surely kill him!"

A woman prays in the chapel: "O, lord, I've never asked you for anything before. But times are hard, so can I please have a win on the National Lottery?" No answer came from on high.

The following week she visits the chapel again. "Lord," she prays, "I haven't heard from you. Have you forgotten me? I only wanted a small win." Again no answer came from on high. She visits the chapel a third time. "Lord," she prays sadly, "I think you've really forgotten me, and I only wanted a small win." But this time a voice does come from heaven and says, "My child, can't you help me a little too? Can't you at least buy one ticket?"

✝ ✝ ✝ ✝ ✝

"Do you think, Molly, should I have put more fire into my sermon at Mass today?" the priest asked his housekeeper. "No, Father," said Molly, "I think you should have put more of your sermon into the fire!"

Some preachers who don't know what to do with their hands should try clamping them over their mouths.

Two nuns were driving through the countryside when they ran out of petrol. They walked to a nearby farmhouse for help and the kindly farmer said that they could siphon some of the petrol from his car. However, they couldn't find anything in which to carry the petrol, until the farmer produced a battered old chamber pot. The nuns filled the pot with petrol, walked back to the car, and began pouring it in. A passing motorist, hardly believing what he saw, stopped and said, "I don't agree with your religion, sisters, but I certainly admire your faith."

Live every day as if it was your last, and one day you'll be right.

Today is the tomorrow that you worried about yesterday.

I'd like to help you out. Which way did you come in?

God so loved the world that he did not send a committee.

✝ ✝ ✝ ✝ ✝

It was All-Ireland Sunday in Croke Park and the crowds had been gathering since early morning. One of the first into the Hogan Stand was a man who had presented two tickets on arrival. With only five minutes to go before the Senior match the seat beside him remained unoccupied. This aroused the curiosity of the person on his other side. "Are you waiting on someone?" he inquired. "Ah, no," replied the man, "we had a death in the family since I bought the tickets. In fact, to tell you the truth, it was my wife that died." "I'm very sorry for your trouble," said the other, "but could you not get anyone else from the family to come along with you?" "Yerrah, not at all, sure they all wanted to go to the funeral!"

✠ ✠ ✠ ✠ ✠

You can't change the past but you can ruin a perfectly good present by worrying about the future.

 ✝ ✝ ✝ ✝ ✝

There is a tombstone in a graveyard in Yorkshire, England, with the following inscription:

Remember, friend, when passing by
As you are now, so once was I.
As I am now, soon you will be.
Prepare for death and follow me.

Someone has written below:

To follow you I'm not content
Until I know which way you went.

An Irish couple were visiting the Holy Land for their Golden Wedding anniversary. When they came to the Sea of Galilee, they noticed a sign which said: BOAT TRIPS ON THE LAKE — £50. "That's very expensive," remarked the husband. "Remember," said the boatman, "Our Lord walked across here." "At those prices," said the husband, "I'm not surprised!"

A farmer's son was out in the fields when a lorry-load of soldiers pulled up on the road nearby. He watched with great interest as they disembarked and fell into formation. Something about these men appealed to him and he decided there and then to enlist in the army. When he broke the news to his father sometime later, the father wasn't at all impressed and tried everything to dissuade him. But to no avail.

The next day the son set off for the Curragh Camp.

At first he found the army life to be altogether new and different, but in time the novelty wore off and he began to yearn for home. Finally he could stick it no longer and he returned home, looking for his old job back again. The father was unyielding. "I warned you and you wouldn't listen," he said. "So let you go back to the Curragh now and soldier on!" Thus the son had no choice but to do just that.

They say that the lowest ebb is the turning of the tide and this was proved true in the case of this farmer's son. Within a short space of time he became an N.C.O. and then progressed rapidly through the ranks until he ended up a captain. One day a letter arrived from his mother with the news that his father had passed on. The letter also sought some money so that Masses could be offered for the happy repose of his soul. This was the son's reply:

"Dear Mother: Thank you for your letter. With regard to your request for some Mass money, here is my response: Number one, if it's a thing that my father has gone to heaven, then he has no need of Masses at all. Number two, if it's a thing that he has gone to hell, then there's no amount of Masses will do him any good. And number three, if it's a thing that he has gone to purgatory, you can tell him that I said he's to soldier on!"

✝ ✝ ✝ ✝ ✝

The Clown's Prayer

*Dear Lord, I thank you for calling me
to share with others
the precious gift of laughter.
May I never forget
that it is your gift and my privilege.
As your children are rebuked in their
self-importance
and cheered in their sadness,
help me to remember
that your foolishness is wiser than human wisdom.*

Traditional

President Robinson was being entertained at the White House by President Clinton. In the Oval Office, she noticed a huge golden telephone, standing in an alcove under a soft light. "What's that for?" she asked. "Oh," said the President coolly, "that's our hotline to heaven." "Direct to God?" "Sure. It's our private line." Mrs. Robinson was intrigued and asked: "How much does it cost to make a call?" "Well, about three thousand dollars a minute," was the President's reply.

Later that year, President Clinton visited Ireland. There, on the wall of Aras an Uachtarain, was a huge silver telephone. "What's that for?" asked the president. "Oh," said Mrs. Robinson, nonchalantly, "that's my personal line to the Almighty." "I see," said Mr. Clinton, "and how much does it cost to make a call?" "About 10p for three minutes," she replied. President Clinton was staggered. "10p! How did you arrange that?" "Ah, well," said Mrs. Robinson, "it's a local call from here!"

"My priest knows much more than your minister," said the little Catholic girl to the little Protestant girl. "Of course he does," came the reply, "that's because you tell him everything in confession!"

A family was entertaining the parish priest for dinner. The hostess, keen to show that they upheld Christian standards in their home, asked her five-year old son to say grace. He looked blank. There was an awkward pause, followed by a reassuring smile from the boy's mother. "Just say what Daddy said at breakfast this morning," she encouraged. Obediently, the boy repeated: "Oh God, we've got that bloomin' parish priest coming for dinner tonight!"

A couple were preparing to celebrate their golden wedding anniversary. The wife went out to have her hair done while the husband offered to tidy the house. During the course of his tidying he came across an old cardboard box with two eggs and a bundle of notes inside. He counted the money and it came to £1,000. As soon as the wife returned he asked her what the box was all about. Immediately her face reddened and then she confessed, "Each time I was unfaithful to you over the past fifty years I put one egg inside that box." "Well," said the husband, "it's not a bad track record. In any case, I'm willing to forgive and forget. But tell me first, what about the £1,000?" The wife further confessed: "Every time I had a dozen eggs, I sold them!"

A visiting priest was puzzled to hear a congregation being admonished with these words: "In future, when I assign a litany as a penance, I don't mean a quick litany." Afterwards, the visitor asked: "Father, what's a 'quick litany'?" The parish priest laughed. "Believe it or not, I happened to be in the rear of the church one evening and an elderly parishioner was praying aloud: 'All the saints on this page, pray for us. All the saints on this page, hear our prayers. From all the things on this last page, deliver us. O Lord'."

A salesman was driving through a very built-up part of town when he noticed a mother and child hurrying somewhere in great distress. The salesman stopped the car, rolled down the window, and asked if anything was wrong. The woman explained that the child had just swallowed a pound coin. "Jump in," said the man, "and I'll drive you to the hospital." "Not at all," said the mother, "I'm bringing him up to the parish priest. He'd get money out of anyone!"

In the days when clergy travelled on horseback, a priest rode up to a farmer's house, dismounted and told a young boy standing nearby to hold the horse while he went in to visit the family. "Indeed and I won't," said the boy cheekily. The priest was flabbergasted. "Do you not realise, young man, that I have the power to stick you to the ground!" "In that case," said the boy, "why don't you stick the auld horse to the ground and we'll both go in!"

† † † † †

The newly-ordained priest arrived at his first appointment in the west of Ireland. In the course of his briefing by the parish priest, he was told that poteen-making was a thing which frequently came up in confession. That evening the new curate was sitting in his confessional, feeling very unsure of himself. After a while someone entered the box and began to confess: "Bless me, Father, for I have sinned. I made 60 gallons of poteen this week." The young priest couldn't figure out what penance to give, so he left the box and ran over to the confessional where the P.P. was hearing. "Father, Father," he gasped, "I have a man who's after making 60 gallons of poteen this week. What will I give him?" With a smile the parish priest said: "You'll give him £3 a bottle and no more!"

Emigration brought a young man from Ireland all the way to New York. Shortly after arriving he sought out an Irish-owned bar and decided to make it his local. He always drank on his own but ordered four beers at at time. Having consumed these he would order another four and then continued to order in fours each time. This puzzled the bartender greatly. "Do you mind me asking," he inquired, "why is that you always order four beers at a time?" "Well," said the man, "there's a very simple explanation really. You see, I have three brothers at home and the night before I left for America we promised each other that whenever we were out for a drink we'd have one for each other and one for ourselves." The bartender was greatly impressed by such an example of brotherly love.

Some weeks later the same man came into the bar again and this time ordered only three beers. The bartender presumed that one of the brothers at home must have died and offered his sympathy. "What for?" asked the man. "Well," explained the bartender, "I see that one of your brothers has died." "Not at all," said the Irishman, "it's Lent and I'm off the drink!"

Paddy the Irishman, Paddy the Englishman, and Paddy the Scotsman died and went to heaven. They were met by St. Peter at the gate. "How many times were you unfaithful to your wife?" he asked the Scotsman. Paddy the Scotsman replied: "Only twice." "Good enough," said St. Peter, "take this Ford Escort and drive on into eternity." The Englishman was next in line and he was asked the same question. The reply came: "Only five times." "Alright," said St. Peter, "take this Ford Fiesta and drive on into eternity." The Irishman was next and he too was asked the same question. Paddy was most emphatic in his reply: "Not once was I unfaithful to my wife," he said. "I'll take your word for it," said St. Peter, "now you take this Rolls Royce and drive on after the rest."

As soon as he caught up with the other two they all stopped to compare cars. The others noticed that the Irishman wasn't a bit happy. "What's wrong with you?" they both asked. "Didn't you get a Rolls Royce?" "I know I did," said Paddy, "but I passed the wife just now and she's on roller skates!"

✠ ✠ ✠ ✠ ✠

✠ ✠ ✠ ✠ ✠

Young Johnny wanted more than anything else in the world to get a mountain bike. He thought of writing to Santa Claus for one but then reckoned that it was too long to wait for Christmas. So he decided to write a letter to God. "Dear God," he began, "I promise to be good for two weeks. Please send me a mountain bike." Shortly after finishing the letter he concluded that he couldn't possibly manage to be good for two whole weeks. So he wrote a second note: "Dear God, I promise to be good for two days. Please send me a mountain bike." This too seemed to be promising the impossible, so he tried a third time: "Dear God, I promise to be good for two hours. Please send me a mountain bike." Still young Johnny knew that his plan was bound to falter. Nearing desperation, he hit on a different idea. He took down a statue of Our Lady, wrapped it carefully in a towel, and placed it in the top drawer of his bedside locker. Then he began to write again: "Dear God, you better send me a mountain bike or you'll never see your mother alive again!"

An old Dublin lady went to confession. She was waiting so long to be heard that she became drowsy and fell fast asleep. After about ten minutes the slide went across with a bang and the old lady awakened suddenly. At the top of her voice she said, "Give us a baby Power and a bottle of stout, and turn on the light in the snug while you're at it!"

In darkest Africa there was a river infested with crocodiles. On the other side was a tribe which various missionaries wanted to convert. However, nobody was willing to take the risk of crossing the river. Then along came a group of Irish priests who waded across the river without any difficulty and without coming to any harm. Some time later they revealed their secret. "We wore T-Shirts", one explained, "bearing the words *England - World Cup Champions 1994*. And sure not even a crocodile was willing to swallow that!"

Nervous breakdowns are hereditary: we get them from our children.

The Reverend Ian Paisley walked into a ward in the Royal Victoria Hospital in Belfast. He looked to the left and saw seven beds with the letter "P" over them. He looked to the right and saw three beds with the letters "RC" over these. Then he turned to the nurse and said: "This is what I like to see: seven Protestants and three Roman Catholics." "You're all wrong," said the nurse, "that's seven for porridge and three for rice crispies!"

A venerable pope died and went straight to heaven. Shortly after arriving he was shown to his quarters. Taking his key, he opened the door of his room and, while it was comfortable, it was small and ordinary. Further along the patio he noticed a sumptuous suite, occupied by a banker. "This is odd," thought His Holiness. "I shall speak to the clerk to see if there isn't some mistake." Finding the clerk, he said that on earth he had occupied a sumptuous palace from which he had guided millions of devoted parishioners. He pointed out that the banker had a luxurious and spacious suite, all of which was hardly fitting. "Is there a mistake?" he asked. "No mistake," said the heavenly clerk. "You see you're the 177th pope we've had, but this is the first time we've had a banker!"

A £5 note and a 2p piece met one time in a person's pocket. They immediately struck up a conversation about places they had been and things they had seen. The £5 note was the first to speak: "I've been to bars, cinemas, casinos, theatres, restaurants and hotels all over the world." Then the 2p piece spoke: "I'm afraid I can't say that I was ever in any of those grand places. All I can say is that I never missed Mass on a Sunday!"

A visiting preacher had just given a riveting sermon at the parish mission. Afterwards a lady from the congregation came to congratulate him. "That was a marvellous homily," she said, "and I really admired the way you paused every so often. You had us all wondering what you were going to say next." "That's funny," said the preacher, "so was I!"

Two men were passing the local Protestant church. They stopped to read the notice board outside. At the bottom it said: "Holy Communion: Last Sunday of the Month." This caused one to remark to the other: "There you are, there's cutbacks everywhere!"

The convent was on retreat. On the first morning the priest who was giving the retreat suggested an unusual exercise for the Sisters. He asked them to spend a half-hour in contemplation and to decide on what one thing in the convent chapel they would like to be and why.

At a subsequent sharing session one sister told how she would like to be a candle and thus bring light and warmth to the world. A second revealed how she would like to be a Bible and thus spread good news everywhere she went. A third sister confessed that she would like to be an altar cloth. When asked why, she said: "Because then I would get a kiss from Father each day at Mass!"

✠ ✠ ✠ ✠ ✠

A great story has been doing the rounds in Northern Ireland for quite some time now. It tells of a telephone conversation on live radio between a D.J. and one of his female listeners. "Are you married?" asks the D.J. "Yes," comes the reply. "How many children have you?" he continues. "Two," says the lady. "And what are they?" "They're both Protestants!"

✝ ✝ ✝ ✝ ✝

A certain evangelist was so successful at his work that he managed to convert his own horse! This prompted him to think that he could extend his "ministry to animals" by taking his horse to the local market and exchanging it for another. A farmer came riding by on a very old horse, and the evangelist begged him to swap animals. The farmer looked at the fine fettle of the evangelist's horse and agreed, delighted with his bargain. As he mounted his new steed, the evangelist explained to him about the horse's religious zeal. The farmer looked at him incredulously.

"It's no good shouting 'Giddyup!' or 'whoa there, boy!'" the evangelist went on. "To start, you have to shout, 'Praise the Lord! Alleluia!' and to stop, you have to shout, 'Amen!'"

The farmer began to suspect that he was listening to a nutcase, but he decided to humour him. The horse was in excellent condition and he accepted. As the evangelist trotted away on the farmer's ageing horse, the farmer shouted "Giddyup!" to his steed. There was still no reaction. He whipped the horse, but there was still no reaction.

"Get up the yard!" he screamed, digging in his heels. The horse refused to budge. The farmer scratched his head.

"Perhaps that old preacher wasn't so crazy after all," he thought. "Oh, well, no harm in trying." He took a deep breath and shouted, "Praise the Lord! Alleluia!" Immediately the horse galloped off. The astonished farmer clung for dear life as it sped along the road.

On and on the pious creature went, crossing fields and jumping gates. At last, hearing the sound of the sea in the distance, the farmer knew that they were approaching the ocean cliffs.

"Whoaa there, boy!" he called. "Whoaa there!" He yanked the reins. The horse sped on regardless. "Silly me," thought the farmer, "I have to say that special word!"

"Blessing!" he shouted. "No, that's wrong. Faith!" he called, urgently. "No, that's not right either."

The sound of the sea came nearer, and try as he might, the farmer could not remember the right religious word. Suddenly, within yards of the cliff edge, he remembered.

"Amen!" he screamed. The horse stopped, with only inches to spare. The farmer mopped his brow and, lifting his eyes to heaven in gratitude, murmured: "Praise the Lord! Alleluia!"

The Parish Priest became ill on a Saturday evening, just as he was preparing for Mass. He thought the sickness might pass, but instead it grew worse. So he called the sacristan to the presbytery and asked him to go and make the following announcements:

1. The parish priest is sick and it won't be a mortal sin for anyone to miss Mass this weekend.

2. Next Sunday is the third Sunday of the month and the monthly collection will be taken up.

3. This Thursday is the feast of Saints Peter and Paul and the annual collection for the pope will be taken up.

4. Maggie Jane and Willie Joe are to be married in this church and anyone knowing of any reason why they shouldn't is to contact the parish priest.

5. A brown parcel was found at the back of the church and the owner may collect it at the presbytery.

The sacristan promised to do as the P.P. had asked. However, he was a very absent-minded individual and by the time he reached the church he really wasn't sure of what to say. Still, he decided to give it his best shot and this is what he announced:

1.   Everyone is sick and it'll be a mortal sin for the parish priest to miss Mass this weekend.

2.   Next Sunday is the thirteenth Sunday of the the month and the annual collection will be taken up by the pope.

3.   This Thursday is the feast of Maggie Jane and Willie Joe.

4.   Peter and Paul are to be married in this church and anyone wanting to know why will find the answer in a brown parcel at the back of the church.

The Reverend Ian Paisley was spotted in the centre of Belfast, holding a bicycle in the air. When asked by an onlooker what he was doing he replied, "I'm holding a Raleigh!"

✝ ✝ ✝ ✝ ✝

The story is told of the fellow who hadn't been to Confession for close on 40 years. One day he happened to be in Dublin and plucked up the courage to go.

He began in the customary fashion: "Bless me, Father, for I have sinned. It's near 40 years since my last Confession, Father."

Then, with some difficulty he recounted the deeds he had done. No stone was left unturned as he endeavoured to make a clean sweep. Even the most trivial misdemeanours got a mention.

After about 15 minutes of "telling all" he asked the priest for absolution. His request was met with total silence from the other side. Again he asked for forgiveness, and again there was nothing forthcoming. Finally, in desperation he begged his confessor to take away his sins.

Now his pleading eyes began to focus and he could see that the priest wasn't there at all. He could also see that there was a little old lady on the far side with her right ear firmly pressed against the grille.

"Where's the priest?" the man inquired.

"I don't know for sure," came the reply, "but if he's after hearing half of what I just heard I'd say he's gone for the police!"

✝ ✝ ✝ ✝ ✝

The Value of a Smile

It costs nothing but creates much.

It enriches those who receive without impoverishing those who give.

None are so well off that they can get along without it, and none so poor but are richer for its benefits.

It creates happiness in the home, fosters goodwill in business, and is the countersign of friends.

It is rest to the weary, daylight to the discouraged, sunshine to the sad, and nature's best remedy for trouble.

Yet it cannot be bought, begged, borrowed, or stolen, for it is something that is no earthly good to anybody until it is given away.

To smile then is to look at others with the eyes of Christ. To know how to love them and smile at them, through our tears if need be, is to breathe in advance the atmosphere of heaven.

(SMA Fathers, Cork)

✠ ✠ ✠ ✠ ✠

✝ ✝ ✝ ✝ ✝

An elderly lady embarks on her annual pilgrimage to Lourdes. In the duty-free shop, before the return journey, she can't resist the temptation to purchase several bottles of vodka and gin. Then she realises that she has far exceeded her duty-free allowance. But she hits on a novel idea. She decides to empty some of the bottles into a number of containers for holy water.

Back in Ireland the lady is called to one side by a seasoned customs official who straightaway begins to examine the containers of "holy water". He unscrews the cap, smells first, then tastes a little. "This isn't holy water," he exclaims. "It's gin!" The elderly lady throws her arms up in the air and shouts: "Glory be to God!" It's another miracle!"

TAKE TIME TO LAUGH… IT IS THE MUSIC OF THE SOUL.